YOU CHOOSE

RUMPELSTILTSKIN

AN INTERACTIVE FAIRY TALE ADVENTURE

by Eric Braun

illustrated by
Alan Brown

CAPSTONE PRESS
a capstone imprint

You Choose Books are published by Capstone Press,
1710 Roe Crest Drive, North Mankato, Minnesota 56003
www.mycapstone.com

Library of Congress Cataloging-in-Publication Data
Library of Congress Catagloging-in-Publication data is available on the Library of
Congress website.
978-1-5157-8775-4 (library binding)
978-1-5157-8777-8 (paperback)
978-1-5157-8779-2 (eBook PDF)

Editorial Credits
Michelle Hasselius, editor; Lori Bye, designer; Bob Lentz, art director;
Gene Bentdahl, production specialist

Image Credits
Shutterstock: solarbird, background

Printed in China
264

Table of Contents

About Your Adventure

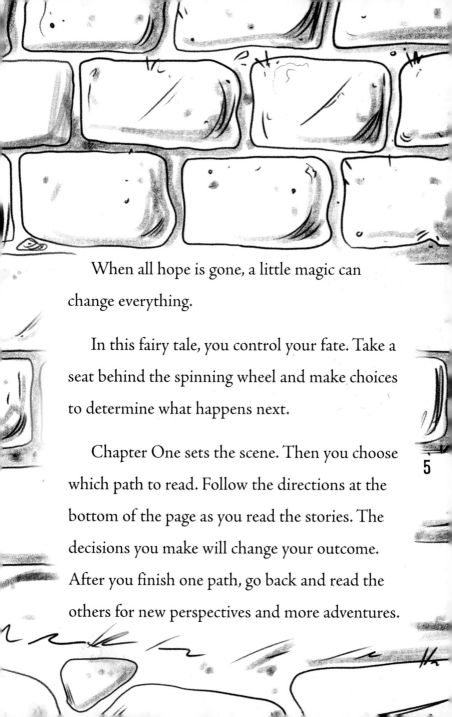

When all hope is gone, a little magic can change everything.

In this fairy tale, you control your fate. Take a seat behind the spinning wheel and make choices to determine what happens next.

Chapter One sets the scene. Then you choose which path to read. Follow the directions at the bottom of the page as you read the stories. The decisions you make will change your outcome. After you finish one path, go back and read the others for new perspectives and more adventures.

Let Me Out!

YOU are inside a locked, dark room. The cruel slam of the door echoes in your ears as you look around. Getting out won't be easy. No back doors, no windows. You shake the door handle, but it doesn't move.

Now what? you wonder to yourself.

The king has demanded the impossible. Complete what is asked of you or suffer the consequences. But all is not lost. You may have a trick or two up your sleeve.

TO BE A CITIZEN OF A FUTURISTIC UNDERWATER WORLD,
TURN TO PAGE 11.

TO BE A STUDENT AT A WACKY MIDDLE SCHOOL,
TURN TO PAGE 43.

TO BE A MAGICAL BUT LONELY LITTLE MAN,
TURN TO PAGE 75.

CHAPTER 2

The Air in There

The future has arrived, and it's not pretty. For years you heard about how global climate change was damaging the world. Someday, the experts warned, you won't recognize Earth.

Well someday is now. Sea levels have risen so far that land is disappearing. The cities that haven't submerged are overcrowded, and the air is filthy with pollution. The government, rebel gangs, and ordinary people fight violently over turf. To escape the chaos, some desperate communities have built bubbles underwater.

These bubble cities get fresh air through pipes that run to the surface of the water. But the air is still dirty, and the population inside your bubble is outgrowing what the pipes can provide.

Your father is a seaweed miller, but he always wished to be something more. A hero. Spinning seaweed into cotton yarn for clothing used to be an important job. But with oxygen getting short, it seems ridiculous. Who cares about nice clothes when it's so hard to breathe?

That's why the king of your bubble got so excited when Father said you could spin seaweed straw into oxygen. Down here oxygen is more valuable than gold. The king could make a fortune selling fresh oxygen to the people. Before you could say fool's gold, the greedy king locked you inside a small, dark room with a spinning wheel and piles of seaweed.

"Turn this seaweed into oxygen by morning," the king said, "or you will die."

You fall to the cold, hard floor and begin to cry. It's hopeless. There is nothing to do but wait for the guards to return by morning. They will take you away and . . . it's too awful to think about.

Suddenly there is a knock at the door. "Why are you crying?" says a gentle, sympathetic voice.

You put your hand on the door and reply, "I am to be killed in the morning."

"Maybe I can help you," the voice whispers.

13

Like magic the door knob that was locked a moment ago turns. In walks a small man with a large nose and pale, warty skin. He is ugly except for his bright, playful eyes.

TO RUN PAST THE MAN AND OUT THE DOOR,
TURN TO PAGE 14.

TO LET THE MAN HELP YOU,
TURN TO PAGE 16.

The little man stands in the doorway,
blocking your way out. You look into the
hallway — no guards. The coast is clear.

"Why are you crying?" the man asks again.

"Come over here by the spinning wheel," you
say, "and I'll tell you."

If you can draw him away from the doorway,
you can make a run for it. The little man steps
into the room, but he stops when he sees you
eyeing the hallway.

"You want to run," he says. "I understand. But you will never make it — guards are everywhere."

"Who are you?" you ask. "How did you manage to get in?"

"I can help you," he says. "But you have to trust me. And you have to give me something in exchange."

TO TRUST THE LITTLE MAN,
TURN TO PAGE 16.

TO RUN FOR IT LIKE YOU PLANNED,
TURN TO PAGE 23.

"Why are you to be killed?" the little man asks. You explain what happened, and he shakes his head. "Aren't people greedy?" he says.

"Yes," you say sadly. "But can you help me, like you said?"

The little man looks at the seaweed straw and then at the spinning wheel. He walks over and picks up one of the straws, sifting it through his fingers. Behind the spinning wheel, a rubber hose leads to a steel tank. He raps the tank with his bony knuckles. *Bong! Bong!*

"The oxygen goes in here?" he asks.

You nod.

"I can spin this seaweed straw into oxygen," he says. He turns and gives you a bright grin.

Your heart inflates in your chest. "Oh, thank you. Thank you!"

FULL

"I will help you. But what will you give me in exchange?" the little man asks. You look at him with surprise, and he says, "Like I said, people are greedy."

You finger the necklace at your throat. Your father gave it to you for your birthday long ago, and it reminds you of simpler days. Of course your father is the one who got you into this mess. You don't feel very sentimental about his gift right now.

TO GIVE THE MAN YOUR NECKLACE,
TURN TO PAGE 19.

TO TRY TO TRICK THE MAN INTO DOING THE WORK FOR FREE,
TURN TO PAGE 21.

You unclasp the necklace and hand it to the man. Without even looking at the beautiful piece of jewelry, he stuffs it into a pocket in his cloak and sits at the spinning wheel. He reaches for the seaweed without a word and begins fitting bunches onto the wheel. He steps on the pedal and begins to pump it. As he does, the wheel turns — slowly at first, then faster. *Squeak! Squeak!* the machine protests. But as it settles into a rhythm, the sound turns into *hush, hush, hush, hush.*

You watch the wheel. As it spins the seaweed bunches tighten and stretch into ropes. The ropes twist into strands of yarn, flowing around a smaller wheel on the machine. The seaweed yarn seems to dissolve in a cloud of steam as it feeds into the rubber hose. A film of frost forms on the hose as the seaweed — now oxygen — flows into the steel tank.

All night the little man works, grinning with glee at his strange magic. The pile of seaweed shrinks. The needle on the oxygen tank meter rises: Empty ... ¼ tank ... ½ tank ... ¾ tank ... FULL.

TURN TO PAGE 24.

Suddenly an idea occurs to you. "No thanks," you tell the little man.

He frowns. "No thanks?"

"Right. I'll do it myself," you say.

"But you *can't* do it!" he says.

"Why should I believe *you* can do it?" you ask.

"Just watch!" he huffs.

Sitting at the wheel, the little man threads bunches of seaweed onto the wheel and begins to spin it. The seaweed thins out and disappears through the hose under a cloud of magical steam and into the tank. You smile as you watch the pile of seaweed straw disappear. The tank is filmed with frost, and the meter reads: "Full."

21

TURN THE PAGE.

"Amazing," you say. "What other magic can you do?"

"I can do many things," the man says, waving his hand with an air of mystery.

TO PAY THE MAN AND WAIT FOR THE KING,
TURN TO PAGE 24.

TO ASK THE MAN TO PUT A SPELL ON THE KING,
TURN TO PAGE 27.

"Sorry," you say, "but I'm not waiting around here to find out what happens when the king comes back."

You move for the doorway, but it magically closes. You grab the door knob, but it is locked again. You spin to face the man.

"Allow me to help you," he says.

"Why should I trust you?" you ask. "I don't even know your name."

"What choice do you have?" he asks.

You wear a necklace with a golden pendant in the shape of a seaweed stalk — a gift from your father. It pains you to give it away, but you lay it in the man's bony hand.

23

"Where do you want to go?" he asks.

TO GO TO THE MAINLAND, TURN TO PAGE 38.

TO HIDE IN THE BUBBLE CITY, TURN TO PAGE 41.

When you awake in the morning, the little man is gone. So is the seaweed. Only a few seeds remain. The king enters the room and examines the tank.

"Unbelievable!" he says, touching the cold steel.

Immediately the king takes you to another room. It has even more seaweed straw than before. Another, bigger tank sits nearby.

"Spin this seaweed into oxygen," he says, "and I will make you a senator of our bubble city. If you do not, it will be death."

But when the little man returns that night, you have nothing to trade him. "I've given you everything I have," you say, defeated.

"Then I will take your firstborn child," the man says.

It's a horrible thought. But you think, you don't plan on having children. Even if you do, it will be years from now. Surely the man will forget by then. Besides if you say no, the king will certainly kill you.

Reluctantly you agree, and the little man does his magic. When the king returns, he keeps his word and installs you as a senator of the underwater city.

Years pass. You are a good senator, and soon you are appointed to a new position: Secretary of Bubble Integrity. You are wealthy and highly respected. And you even fall in love. When your child is born, you have forgotten all about the deal you made with the little man.

25

TURN THE PAGE.

But one day the man arrives at your home asking for his half of your agreement.

"I can offer you money and power," you say. "Surely you want these things instead?"

"I must demand my rightful payment," he says.

"I won't do it," you say desperately. "I'll have my guards throw you in prison. I'll have them kill you!"

The man laughs. "Do you not remember how powerful my magic is? Your guards can't hurt me. Better to just give me what is mine, and no one will get hurt — including you."

TO REFUSE TO GIVE THE LITTLE MAN YOUR BABY,
TURN TO PAGE 29.

TO BEG THE MAN FOR MERCY,
GO TO PAGE 31.

"I have an idea that will make us lots of money," you say to the little man.

When the king comes to the door in the morning, the little man blows a handful of seaweed dust into his face and says the magic word, "Slumpelstiltskin." The king slumps against the wall and falls sleep.

The little man grabs your hand. "Let's go!"

You sneak down a back staircase and slip out into the dark, underwater morning. As you run along the streets, you ask the stranger his name. He replies, "Never mind."

At his home the nameless man spins seaweed straw into oxygen, which you sell in tanks. For some reason he insists on naming your business Lungfullstiltskin. As natural oxygen becomes more and more scarce, the demand for your product skyrockets. Soon you are a millionaire, and you retire in an underwater mansion.

Over the years you grow fond of the little man. Eventually that fondness turns to love. You marry in a spectacular wedding. As the minister pronounces you husband and wife, the little man raises your veil and whispers his name into your ear.

THE END

TO FOLLOW ANOTHER PATH, TURN TO PAGE 9.

28

You know the man will use his magic to get what he wants. But you don't care.

"You'll never take her!" you scream.

You move to grab your baby from her bassinet, but the little man is too fast. Before you know it, he has her in his arms. The baby, whom you haven't named yet, giggles as the little man tickles her under the chin. Then they both disappear.

You use all your resources as a senator, but the little man and your child are nowhere to be found. For weeks you lay in bed depressed. Finally one night you decide that you need to get as far away as possible. You go to the Surface Subway station and catch a Verti-Train to the Ocean Platform. You have brought nothing with you — no ID, no extra clothing or food, only enough money to get you to the mainland.

You catch a ferry. After a long ride, you arrive in time to see the sun rise over the water. You haven't seen the sun in many years, and you begin to cry. The moment is disrupted by nearby gunfire, and you find a place to hide in a trash-scattered alley.

You don't know what life in the old world will bring for you. But after all that's happened, you no longer want all your wealth and power in the bubble city. It's brought nothing but pain.

THE END

TO FOLLOW ANOTHER PATH, TURN TO PAGE 9.

"Please," you say. "Isn't there something I can do to change your mind?"

The man's bright eyes look at you with pity. "If you can tell me my name," he says, "I will let you keep your child."

You have never thought to ask his name, so you guess. "Timothy?" you say. He shakes his head. "Larry?" Nope. "Big Nose?" Nope. "McGillicuddy?" Nuh-uh.

"I'll give you three days to tell me my name," he says.

You send out messengers to scour the bubble for the names of everyone they meet. They bring back long lists of names.

When the little man returns, you try them all. "Jacob? Ham-hock? Geisel? Malcolm? King Tut?"

No, no, no, no, and no.

On the morning of the third day, a messenger comes to your office. "I heard a man dancing and singing," he tells you. "The man sang a song that went like this:

Merrily the feast I'll make.

Today I'll brew, tomorrow bake.

Merrily I'll dance and sing,

For next day will a stranger bring.

Little does my lady dream,

Rumpelstiltskin is my name!"

Rumpelstiltskin! So that is his name. Later
that day the little man arrives as planned. When
he walks into your office, he is grinning madly.
He is certain that he's won. You can't wait to tell
him his name and wipe that smile off his face.
Part of you wants to punish him for trying to
take your baby. At the same time, you know the
king would have killed you if the man had not
helped you.

33

TO PUNISH HIM, GO TO PAGE 34.

TO SHOW SOME MERCY, GO TO PAGE 37.

You lean forward in your chair, elbows on your desk, and look him in the eye. Your baby sleeps in a crib by your side.

"Is your name . . . John?" you say with a smile.

"No, ma'am," he says, his eyes twinkling. He thinks he has you.

"Is it Tom?" you ask.

"It's not Tom," he says, dancing.

You lean back. You enjoy teasing him. You can't seem to help yourself. Anyway, it is time to end the game. "Well then, your name must be . . . Rumpelstiltskin!"

The man's mouth drops open and his face turns red. "Who told you that?" he cries, and stamps his foot so hard that the room shakes.

Looking down you see that his foot has plunged deep into the floor. You hear a rumbling, and a trickle of water seeps out of the crack around his foot. Rumpelstiltskin grabs onto his leg and pulls. He pulls again. He pulls so hard that he tears himself in two!

Rumpelstiltskin screams in pain, but you can barely hear it over a blaring alarm: *Warning! Warning! The bubble has been breached!*

The floor is already an inch deep in water. People are running and screaming in the hall. You pick up your baby and join them. You are rich and powerful, but right now that doesn't help. You're running for your life like everyone else.

THE END

36

TO FOLLOW ANOTHER PATH, TURN TO PAGE 9.

"Old man," you say, "let's not play games. Your name is Rumpelstiltskin."

His face turns red and he raises his fists over his head in anger. "Aargh!"

"Hold on," you say, holding your hand up. "You helped me once, and so now I will help you. I'm offering you a job in the Senate of another bubble city. You can start a new life there."

You don't know what he will say, but it doesn't matter. You have broken the cycle of selfishness and greed. You have done something generous. Maybe others will follow your example.

37

THE END

TO FOLLOW ANOTHER PATH, TURN TO PAGE 9.

"I want out of this bubble city," you say.

"Done," the little man says.

He takes your hand and opens the door. You slip into the hallway and begin to run. Before your eyes, the hallway turns into a road — a road on land. You're free!

But life on land is not so great. Everyone you meet is miserable. They have soot on their skin. They cough a lot and stare at the ground as they walk. There is fighting in the streets. The only thing that gives people pleasure is TV.

38

That gives you an idea. You propose it to the little man. "Let's make a reality TV show about you," you say. "We'll go around and use your magic to help people who are in trouble. Everyone will love it."

"What will you give me in exchange?" he asks.

You already gave him your necklace. You traded a ring for a place to live. You don't have anything else to give.

"How about your firstborn child?" the man suggests.

I will never have children, you think. It seems like a safe promise to make.

"Deal," you say. You hold out your hand. "Let's shake on it, Mr . . . what's your name anyway?"

THE END

39

TO FOLLOW ANOTHER PATH, TURN TO PAGE 9.

"Just get me out of here," you say. "I don't care where."

The man takes your hand, opens the door, and together you walk out. Instead of walking into the castle hallway, you appear on a street in the bubble city. High above you outside the bubble walls, a school of manta rays swims past.

You're not sure what to do now. Your father endangered your life in exchange for his own fame and fortune. The king wants you dead. The little man took your necklace, but he gave you something in return: Freedom. What else do you want? Riches? Your own bubble city? You twist the ring on your finger. You have one more favor you can ask. You better make it a good one.

THE END

TO FOLLOW ANOTHER PATH, TURN TO PAGE 9.

CHAPTER 3

Too Much Math

There are many rules at Mundane Middle School, but the most important is this: No fun.

Principal King wants to win the National Exceeds Standards Prize for the school. That means every moment has to be spent on learning, practicing, testing, and learning some more. You can't even say the words "pretend," "imagine," or "create." If you do Curriculum Guards will take you to the detention dungeon.

Your dad is the math teacher, Mr. Miller. But he is hoping to be made vice principal. In fact he'd love to become principal of his own school one day. His ambition is what got you into this mess. He told Principal King that you, his star student, could compute reams of math problems without a calculator. Algebra, calculus, geometry, you name it. There's no problem you can't solve. That got Principal King very excited.

"A student like that would be a national star," Principal King exclaimed. "A student like that would surely put the school at the top of the award list. It's like spinning math into pure gold!"

Principal King locked you into this classroom with 100 fat binders full of math problems.

"Solve these all by morning," she said, "or else."

The principal said if you can't solve the problems, a recording would read science chapters in a loud, boring voice over and over. Which will *literally* bore you to death. You bet it won't take long.

You're pretty good at math, but not *that* good. There's no way you can solve all these problems by morning. Suddenly you hear a jingling of keys, and the door opens. In walks a short, bearded man.

"Why are you crying?" he asks.

You tell him the truth. He replies that he can do the math, but you have to give him something in exchange.

TO OFFER YOUR NECKLACE,
TURN TO PAGE 46.

TO ASK FOR PROOF THAT HE CAN DO THE MATH,
TURN TO PAGE 49.

You quickly unclasp the necklace you are wearing and hand it over. The bearded man looks at it and stuffs it into the breast pocket of his shirt. Then without a word he sits at a desk, extracts a pencil from his beard, and opens the first binder. He begins to scribble.

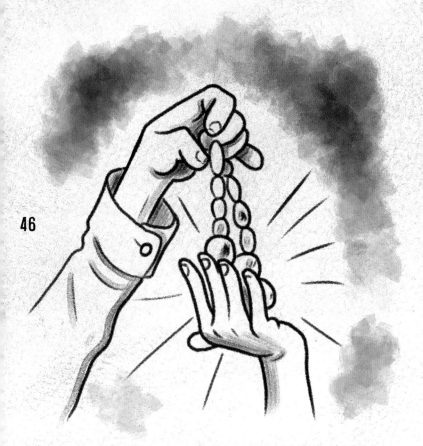

Within ten minutes he tosses the binder to another desk and opens a second one. You open the finished binder. His handwriting is small and very neat. His work is perfect! Every problem is correct. There aren't even any eraser marks.

The second completed binder lands with a *Thump!* next to the first. You check that one, and it too is perfect. You begin to relax. You are not going to die by science lecture after all. You fall asleep as the man continues his work.

When you wake the next morning, the bearded man is gone. Principal King comes in with a cold look on her face and two scowling Curriculum Guards at her side. With each binder she checks, her expression warms a little. By the end she is smiling a big, toothy, evil smile.

47

"You've done well," she says.

TURN THE PAGE.

The principal takes you down the hall to another classroom. This one is stacked with even more math binders than the first.

"Now complete all of *these* problems by morning, or you know what happens," she says.

Shortly after she leaves, you hear the jingle of keys again, and the little man comes in. In exchange for the ring on your finger, he will solve these math problems.

TO GIVE THE MAN YOUR RING,
TURN TO PAGE 50.

TO ASK THE MAN TO LET YOU OUT INSTEAD,
TURN TO PAGE 52.

"Oh, right," you say, "like you can do all this math. *Nobody* can do all this."

"You don't believe me?" the man asks.

"Nope," you say.

"I can do this math with one hand tied behind my back," he says.

"Prove it," you say.

"Hand over the necklace," he says.

"Not until I know you can do it," you say.

The man stares at you and scratches his fluffy beard. Finally he says, "If you don't trust me, I'll just leave. Doesn't matter to me — I'm not the one who's going to die in the morning." He walks toward the door.

49

TO STOP THE MAN AND GIVE HIM YOUR NECKLACE,
TURN TO PAGE 53.

TO TRY TO DO THE MATH YOURSELF,
TURN TO PAGE 54.

You slide the ring off and drop it into the man's open palm. After stuffing it into his beard, he gets to work. By morning the math is complete, the man is gone, and Principal King has returned. After checking the math, she leads you to a third classroom with even more math than the second one. But instead of threatening you, she makes a promise.

"Finish this math by morning, and you will be my new vice principal," she says.

Your father really wants that job. Taking it would be a way to get back at him for getting you into this math mess. But do you really *want* to be a vice principal? That sounds like a lot of work. Of course it might be fun. You would get to tell the other kids what to do.

When the bearded little man returns that night, he offers to do the math. But since you don't have any more jewelry, he asks for your beloved goldfish, Professor Gills.

TO AGREE TO GIVE UP YOUR PET GOLDFISH,
TURN TO PAGE 56.

TO TRY TO MAKE ANOTHER DEAL WITH THE MAN,
TURN TO PAGE 58.

"Principal King is just going to make me do more and more math," you say. "Will you unlock that door and help me get away, please?"

"I can't do that," the bearded man says. "I'm sorry you won't take my offer. Goodbye."

You know you can't do all this math. Instead you stack up two desks, climb on top, and remove a ceiling panel. You climb into the ceiling and crawl as far as you can. When you reach a wall, you kick out a ceiling tile underneath you and lower yourself down.

52

You've landed in a ceramics room. Sitting at a potting wheel spinning a big clay vase is the little bearded man. He looks at you with surprise.

"You're doing art!" you say. "That's not allowed at this school."

TO THREATEN TO TELL THE PRINCIPAL, **TURN TO PAGE 60.**

TO ASK THE MAN TO TEACH YOU ART, **TURN TO PAGE 62.**

"Wait!" you say and hand him your necklace.

The man sits at a desk, opens the first binder, and starts working. You fall asleep. You wake up the next morning just as Principal King walks in.

"Let's see what you've done," Principal King says. She opens the first binder. Shaking her head, she marks something with a red pen. Then she marks something else. Your heart sinks.

"This is terrible," she says, setting it down. "Guards, seize this student."

"Wait!" you say, grabbing the binder. You open it up. On the first page, the man has written a message: *You should have trusted me the first time.*

53

The guards take you by either arm. You just hope the science lessons aren't too boring.

THE END

TO FOLLOW ANOTHER PATH, TURN TO PAGE 9.

The little man shuts the door behind him, and you begin working on the math as fast as you can. Some problems are easy, and you whip through them quickly. But when you get to the harder problems, you realize you're taking too long. You won't get close to finishing by morning.

Principal King comes in bright and early. When she sees you didn't finish, she has you thrown into the detention dungeon with two other kids — a boy and a girl.

After the guards leave, the girl whispers, "We're working on a plan to break out of here. Are you in?"

54

"Yeah, I'm in," you say. "What do we do?"

TO TRY TO GET THE GUARDS TO HELP YOU,
TURN TO PAGE 64.

TO TRY TO GET AWAY ON YOUR OWN,
TURN TO PAGE 67.

You love Professor Gills, but first things first. You have to get out of this classroom alive. Then you can worry about getting your fish back. "OK," you say. "The fish is yours."

The bearded man does the math, and Principal King keeps her promise to make you the vice principal. A few days later, you're in your office writing a new set of school rules. Professor Gills swims happily in his fish bowl on your desk. You hear keys jingle outside the door, and the bearded man walks in.

"I'm here for Professor Gills," he says.

"Please, no," you say. "I'll give you anything!" You start to cry.

"I saved your life," he reminds you. "The least you can do is keep your promise."

57

TO FIGHT TO KEEP YOUR PET,
TURN TO PAGE 69.

TO KEEP BEGGING,
TURN TO PAGE 71.

"Why do you sneak around and do math at night?" you ask. "You are so smart, *you* should be in charge of a school."

"That's true," he says, "I'm very smart, but I don't want to run a school. Enforce the rules, pay the bills, all that stuff. Yuck."

"I could do that stuff for you!" you say. "We'll name the school after you. All we have to do is get out of here."

"Well, it *is* tempting," the man says.

It takes a bit more convincing, but eventually the bearded man sneaks you out. By the next school year, your new school is up and running: Rumpelstiltskin Academy. You win the Exceeds Standards Award in the first year.

It feels great to be in charge of a successful school, but soon you realize that you are not happy. You long to work with your hands, so you take a class on textile spinning. You thread cotton onto a spinning wheel and spin it into thread, which you use to make your own clothes. The work makes you happy, and you're good at it. Soon you hear rumors that your father is boasting about you again.

"That kid could spin straw into gold, I swear," he says.

Uh-oh, you think.

THE END

TO FOLLOW ANOTHER PATH, TURN TO PAGE 9.

You threaten to tell Principal King that the man is being creative on school grounds.

"She will throw you in the detention dungeon," you say. "She will reward me, and let me go."

The man just laughs. "I disappear when I need to. Nobody can find me unless I want them to." He dabs some paint onto his vase, then drops the brush into a bowl of water and fixes you with a dark look. "I tried to help you, but you want to use me just like Principal King is using you. You have learned nothing."

He reaches into the clay vase and pulls out a handful of smoke, which expands and fills the room. You fall unconscious.

You wake up some time later to the sound of a door handle rattling. When you open your eyes, you see that you're back in the room with the math binders. Principal King enters the room with two Curriculum Guards. She checks the binders, but you know none are completed.

Shaking her head in disappointment, Principal King takes you to a small room in the detention dungeon. After the door locks behind her, you hear a speaker crackle and a loud voice.

"Chapter 1: What Is Life? The cell is the basic building block of all living things . . ."

You close your eyes and wait for the sweet release of death.

THE END

TO FOLLOW ANOTHER PATH, TURN TO PAGE 9.

"I want to make art," you say. You feel a flare of excitement fill your stomach. It has been years since you've been allowed to be creative.

The man smiles. "Excellent," he says. "We'll start now."

That night you form a bowl from clay and spin it on the wheel. It's not the most beautiful bowl you've ever seen, but you're proud of it.

Before morning the man magically transports you back to the math room, where he has already completed the math.

62   Principal King makes you vice principal, just as she promised. You are very good at your job. With your help, students' grades are up and misbehavior is down.

Every day after school, you sneak back to the magical art room hidden deep in the school's basement. You make clay pots. You draw. You paint. You play guitar and sing. You love it all.

You are happy in your double life, but one thing bugs you. Though you ask several times, your teacher never tells you his name.

THE END

TO FOLLOW ANOTHER PATH, TURN TO PAGE 9.

"The Curriculum Guards might help us," you say. "I know a couple of them, and they don't like Principal King either. They're just afraid of her."

At dinner time two guards bring in your food. You whisper, "Friends, help us."

The guards look at you, but they act like they didn't hear.

"Let us go," you beg. "Principal King is going to kill us."

One of the guards puts a hand on your shoulder. "We would never dare go against Principal King's orders, unless . . ."

"Unless what?" you ask.

"Do you know the man with the big beard?"

"Yes!" you say. "I know him!"

"He is secretly working to defeat Principal King," the guard says quietly. "The only way we can know if you are on his side is if you tell me his name."

"I don't know his name," you say. "He never told me."

"So he doesn't trust you," the guard says, shaking his head.

"Bring him here," you beg. "I am sure he will tell me his name."

"I'm sorry," the guard says. "Enjoy your dinner. The science lecture begins in an hour. Your death will be painfully boring."

THE END

66

TO FOLLOW ANOTHER PATH, TURN TO PAGE 9.

"We can't trust anyone else," you say. "Let's find our own way out."

You know that the detention dungeon used to be a gym before the middle school became Mundane. The three of you search the walls until you come across a crack. It's an old hidden doorway. Using a hairpin the girl picks the lock. Inside the closet are shelves of gym equipment — including jump ropes! You tie several together, toss the loop overhead into the dark ceiling, and hook it onto a basketball hoop hidden way up in the rafters.

One by one you climb up. You crawl carefully across the beams in the ceiling until you reach an air vent. You climb inside. Half an hour later, you're outside in the cool air.

TURN THE PAGE.

As the three of you part ways, you realize you will never return to the school. You will never see your dad again either. You have nowhere to go. The little man with the big beard was trying to help you. Maybe he could help you again, if only you could find him.

You start walking. After a few minutes, you look up to see a pawn shop called Rumpy's Goods and Gold. You've lived in this town your whole life but never noticed the shop before. You decide to go inside. Maybe you can trade your dad's old watch for something useful.

68

THE END

TO FOLLOW ANOTHER PATH, TURN TO PAGE 9.

You call the Curriculum Guards in from the hall outside your office. "Put him in the detention dungeon!" you say.

The guards move toward the little man. When they try to seize him, their hands grasp only air. You look at your desk and see the little man grabbing Professor Gill's bowl.

"He's over here!" you say, but once again the guards are too slow. The man vanishes and so does your fish.

You hear a cackling laugh in the hallway. But when you rush out of the office, there is nobody there. The man and your fish are gone.

The rest of the day, you burn with anger. Your father walks by your office, and you just glare at him. He's the reason Professor Gills is gone.

You begin to secretly talk the students into purposely failing their tests. When they do Principal King receives a Needs Improvement designation and is fired.

You're the principal now. You fire your dad. Your school will be fun *and* successful. But you need a new math teacher. Hmm, the bearded man would actually be good at that. You wonder if he would be interested in the job. Of course he'll be hard to find. You don't even know his name.

THE END

TO FOLLOW ANOTHER PATH, TURN TO PAGE 9.

You keep crying, and the man begins to feel sorry for you. "I'll give you a chance," he says. "If you can guess my name in three days, you can keep your fish."

You thank him, and he leaves. Immediately you call six of your friends out of class.

"Get on your bikes and scour the town," you say. "Look for a short man with a big beard and find out his name."

The students set off. For two days they find nothing. Then one tells you of a man singing by a campfire in the woods. His song went like this:

Today I sing, tomorrow dance,

For the vice principal has no chance.

To keep the fish and win this game,

For Rumpelstiltskin is my name!

When the man returns on the third day, you say, "Your name is Rumpelstiltskin!"

"How did you know that?" Rumpelstiltskin screams.

He stamps the ground, and his foot punches through the floor. Still screaming, Rumpelstiltskin tries to pull himself out. Instead he tears himself into two equal halves, like a math problem with no remainder.

In the end your school only receives a Meets Standards Award instead of an Exceeds Standards Award. Principal King is furious.

"Obviously I was too easy on everyone this year," she says. "Next year I'll be really strict."

THE END

TO FOLLOW ANOTHER PATH, TURN TO PAGE 9.

CHAPTER 4

The Strange Little Man

Life is lonely when you are an ugly, magical hermit. You live in a hut outside of town, away from everyone. It's not that you hate people. It's just that people tend to laugh at the way you look. Or they are afraid of your magic. Or they complain about your smell. So you keep to yourself.

Sometimes though your magic tells you when someone is in trouble. When that happens you go to them. It's a chance to talk with someone. It's a chance to help. Once in a while, someone actually appreciates you.

That's what happens tonight after the miller's daughter is thrown into that room with all that straw. She needs your help.

When you get inside the room, you tell her that you can spin the straw into gold and save her life. But your magic will not work unless you receive something in exchange. The girl offers you her necklace. You drop it in your pocket and sit at the spinning wheel. Soon a thread of pure gold begins to feed off the wheel and fall into a basket.

The following night she needs you again. You return to spin even more straw into gold. In exchange she gives you a ring.

When you return the third night, she has nothing left to offer you. But if you spin the final batch of straw into gold, she will become the queen. When she does she will be able to give you almost anything.

The promise of a future gift is enough to make your magical power work. But what should you ask for?

TO ASK FOR A GOLD STATUE OF YOURSELF,
TURN TO PAGE 78.

TO ASK FOR THE QUEEN'S FRIENDSHIP,
TURN TO PAGE 79.

You say, "I want a life-size golden statue of myself. Display it in the market square so everyone will know that I am a great man."

"It's a deal," the girl says.

You sit at the spinning wheel one last time and spin the roomful of straw into a huge tangle of golden thread. A few months later, after the girl has been installed as queen, you return to the castle.

"It's time for my statue to be made," you say.

The girl agrees but then adds, "I want my necklace and ring back. Those were gifts from my mother, and they're important to me."

TO GIVE THE JEWELRY BACK,
TURN TO PAGE 82.

TO REFUSE,
TURN TO PAGE 83.

78

"Do you know what I'd really like? I'd like to be invited over to the castle for dinner once a month. I'd like to have friends. Life as a hermit is so lonely."

The girl makes a face like she just sucked a lemon. "Uh," she says. "I don't think so."

This makes you furious. You are not asking for much, and the king will kill her if the straw isn't spun into gold. You may be ugly, but you need friends just like anybody else does. In anger you ask for something that you know will really hurt her.

"Fine," you say. "I'll take your firstborn child instead. That's my final offer."

The girl's mouth drops in horror. You remind her that her only other choice is to be killed by the king.

"All right," she says sadly. "I will simply never have a child."

You spin the final pile of straw into gold, and you leave. Back at your cottage, you listen for cries in the night. They come to you on currents of magical airwaves. Finally years later you hear what you've been waiting for. A baby boy is crying in the girl's arms.

The next morning you show up at the castle. But when you demand the baby, the young queen does not remember you.

You remind her of your deal, and she wails, "No! You cannot have my baby!"

You feel a bit sorry for the queen. On the other hand, she refused to even invite you for dinner. She got herself into this mess. She is selfish and mean and probably will be a mean, selfish mother. If you had a child, you would love it and teach it to be kind.

81

TO GIVE THE QUEEN A CHANCE TO GET OUT OF THE DEAL,
TURN TO PAGE 84.

TO DEMAND THE CHILD,
TURN TO PAGE 86.

You give her the necklace and ring back. You don't care about them anymore — they were just to make the magic work. The statue will be more important anyway. It will truly honor you.

"Artisans have already completed your statue," the girl says. "It will be unveiled tomorrow." As you turn to leave, she touches your shoulder gently. "Thank you, sir. You are a good man."

No one has ever said something so kind to you. It warms your heart. Leaving the castle you can't help but smile. Even in bed that night, you still feel her warm hand on your shoulder.

82

Then the warm feeling turns cold. You hear her crying again. Does she need help?

TO GO TO THE CASTLE NOW,
TURN TO PAGE 88.

TO TALK TO THE QUEEN TOMORROW,
TURN TO PAGE 89.

"I'm sorry," you say. "Those trinkets were the price of magic — and the price for your life. I won't return them now."

"Fine," she says sadly. "Work begins tomorrow on your statue."

You head home and arrange the necklace and the ring on a shelf next to other trinkets you have received to help people. There are many: A wolf's tooth necklace, a crystal teardrop ornament, a child's painting, and more. When the statue is complete, it will be a public version of this trophy shelf. Everyone will know that you are a hero.

But after the statue is revealed, you realize that you are still very lonely. You feel the same way you felt before you met the miller's daughter. Not even a grand statue will change that.

THE END

TO FOLLOW ANOTHER PATH, TURN TO PAGE 9.

You come up with a great idea. "If you can guess my name within three days, you can keep the baby," you tell her.

It's genius, you think. You can return every day and let her guess. Of course she will never figure out your very unusual name. After a few days of fun and games, you will get the baby after all.

The queen throws out a few guesses right away. "Is it David? Horace? Ronald? Mortimer?" she asks.

"No, no, all of them no," you say. "I will return tomorrow to hear more names."

When you return the next day, she has many more guesses. They are all wrong. The following day you return again, and again she is unable to guess your name. As you go home that evening, you begin thinking about raising a son. You can't wait! You're not used to feeling this good, and a strange urge comes over you — you want to sing and dance.

85

TO SING ABOUT YOUR HAPPY FUTURE,
TURN TO PAGE 92.

TO DANCE TO AN OLD PARTY SONG,
TURN TO PAGE 94.

"No," you say. "I'm taking the baby."

The queen lets out a great cry of anguish as you take the infant from her hands. When you get the little boy home, he is crying too.

He must be hungry, you think. You feed him some boiled root vegetables and salted meat, but he spits all of it out. Then he cries and cries.

It stinks in here. That's why the baby cries, you think. So you clean the hut from top to bottom until it sparkles. But the baby keeps crying.

I know, he must be bored, you think. So you make a baby toy out of an old wad of string and a dirty cloth. You wave the toy in front of him, but he keeps crying. No matter what, HE JUST KEEPS CRYING.

You try to think about the good times to come. When the boy is older, you will travel and do magic together. You will play catch in the yard. But it doesn't work. In the end you realize you don't actually like babies. In the morning you decide that you will return him to the queen. There's a reason you are a hermit.

THE END

TO FOLLOW ANOTHER PATH, TURN TO PAGE 9.

You appear at the queen's door and ask, "Why are you crying?"

She puts a finger to her lips and says, "Shhh." She invites you into the castle and tells you why she is sad. "I'm trapped in a life I don't want."

Even though the queen is wealthy, life is not what she thought it would be. The king treats her poorly and only cares about gold.

"I am so lonely," she says. "But I'm afraid to run away. The king will hunt me down."

"I know what it is like to be lonely," you tell her. "Let me help."

88

TO HELP THE QUEEN RUN AWAY,
TURN TO PAGE 96.

TO COME UP WITH ANOTHER IDEA,
TURN TO PAGE 98.

You will see the queen tomorrow. You go to bed, and soon the crying stops. In the morning you get dressed and head to the castle. You knock, but the queen doesn't answer. Instead an old servant woman opens the door.

"I am here to see the queen," you say.

The woman lowers her head. "Dear sir, I am sorry to inform you that the queen is dead."

"What?" you ask. "What happened?"

The servant looks around. "The king demanded to know why a statue was being built in the square. The queen said it was to honor a little man who had helped her," she whispers. "The king then ordered her to tell him the little man's name, but the queen couldn't. The king threatened her life, so the queen took a horse and rode into the forest, meaning to run away.

The servant continues. "The king sent hunters after the queen. He gave them orders to kill her, and I'm afraid that is what they did."

You are shocked and ashamed. You should have gone to the castle last night. You could have helped her.

At the market square a band plays a song, and someone pulls the cover away from your statue. It shows you as proud and strong. But you don't feel proud or strong.

You glance at the bottom of the statue where your name should be. It's labeled "strange little man." You begin to weep. Every time you see it, you will be reminded that your name could have saved a friend.

THE END

TO FOLLOW ANOTHER PATH, TURN TO PAGE 9.

90

You leap and dance by the flickering fire and sing a song of pure joy:

No more loneliness, no more plight,

I'll have my own family tomorrow night.

For no chance will the lady claim,

That Rumpelstiltskin is my name!

You notice a rustling in the forest, but it's probably just some squirrels running around. You return to the castle for the final time, ready to claim your baby. First the queen guesses your name is Arnold. Then she guesses Willis.

"Wrong!" you say cheerfully.

"Well then, I guess your name must be Rumpelstiltskin," the queen says.

Your smile slips off your face, and you feel your insides turn cold. "The devil told you that!" you say.

The queen just smiles. It makes you angry. You stamp your foot on the ground so hard that it plunges right through the floor. You can't seem to get it out.

TO ASK FOR HELP,
TURN TO PAGE 100.

TO TRY TO PULL YOURSELF OUT,
TURN TO PAGE 102.

You dance to a song that your mother used to sing to you a century ago. You have fond memories of your mother, and you miss her tonight.

When you return to the castle the following day, the queen makes several more guesses at your name. None of the guesses are correct, and you take the baby away. You raise the boy to be kind and teach him magic. The two of you grow very close. It's everything you thought it would be. You play catch. You watch funny movies together. You love being a dad.

94

When the boy is a teenager, he hears a voice crying in the night. You hear it too. It's his mother. He seems to know this, though you don't tell him.

"Father, I need to go to her," he says to you.

And so he puts on his best clothes and sets out for the castle. You watch him leave, and part of you is happy for him. He deserves to know his mother, and you hope he will love her as much as you loved your own mother. You feel bad that you kept them apart, but not too bad. After all the magic makes the decisions, not you.

THE END

TO FOLLOW ANOTHER PATH, TURN TO PAGE 9.

You go to the spinning wheel and spin the straw into two disguises. Now you both look like castle servants. Together you walk out the front door and into the night.

"You are free," you say.

The queen looks around, and then turns back to you. "What should I do now? I've never been on my own before."

"You can do anything," you say, "but you must avoid the king. If he finds you, he will put you to death for betraying him."

"Can I hide at your house?" she asks.

You agree, and the two of you return to your hut. Over dinner you discuss her future. Maybe she will flee to another city. Maybe she will stay with you. She is safe here, and you tell her she is welcome.

The queen decides to go to the nearby town and start a new life for herself. Before she leaves she turns to you and says, "You have saved my life, and I don't even know your name. Please tell me so I can thank you properly."

"Well . . .," you say.

THE END

TO FOLLOW ANOTHER PATH, TURN TO PAGE 9.

"If I sneak out of here, I'll live the rest of my life on the run," she says. "I'll always be worried that the king will find me."

"Well," you say reluctantly. "There is another option."

"We have to get rid of the king for good," the queen says.

You nod, surprised that she has guessed so quickly.

You steal a dagger from the weaponry, and together you sneak into the parlor where the king is playing video games. As the queen sneaks up behind him, the king jumps up and grabs her wrist. Then he sees you.

"What's going on here?" the king demands. He calls his guards, who rush in and grab you by the arms before you can cast a spell.

The queen panics. "He made me do it," she says, pointing at you. "He used his magic to put a spell on me."

"What?" you yelp. "I was helping you!"

She shakes her head. "It's a lie," she tells the king.

The king has you thrown into a cell. Tomorrow he says you will be killed. Of course as soon as he leaves, you use your magic to escape. You realize he will send hunters to find you, so you do not return to your hut. Instead you head deep into the forest, deeper than any person has gone. You are free, but you are lonelier than ever.

THE END

TO FOLLOW ANOTHER PATH, TURN TO PAGE 9.

This is embarrassing. "A little help here?" you say.

The queen, laughing, calls two guards over. They grab you by the arms and lift you out. Your boot is stuck in the crack, and you reach down to fish it out. Your face is hot with humiliation.

With one bare foot, you turn to leave, but the queen says your name again. "Rumpelstiltskin, won't you stay?" she asks.

"You want me to stay?" you ask in disbelief.

"Yes," she says. "You are funny. You're fun to have around. Plus," she adds kindly, "I never properly thanked you for saving my life. Join us for dinner, won't you?"

The warmth in your face remains, but now it is from happiness. You have made a friend.

THE END

TO FOLLOW ANOTHER PATH, TURN TO PAGE 9.

Tears stream down your face — tears of pain, tears of embarrassment and rejection, tears of anger. All the feelings you've been keeping inside all these years come rushing to the surface.

In your rage you grab onto your leg and pull. It doesn't budge, so you pull harder. It is still stuck in the floor. You cast a magical spell and give another tug. This time you feel something give way. It is something in the very center of you.

You tug a final time, and an awful tearing sound fills your ears. You realize — too late — that you are tearing your very self in half.

"Aaaaarrrr!" you scream.

The queen screams too. So do the royal guards in the room and the baby too.

You try to stop, but your spell is too strong. Suddenly you are holding half of your body in your hand.

"Get him out of here!" the queen screams to her guards.

Me and my temper, you think. It's the last thought you have.

THE END

TO FOLLOW ANOTHER PATH, **TURN TO PAGE 9.**

CHAPTER 5

A Brief History of Rumpelstiltskin

Researchers believe that the origins of Rumpelstiltskin go back about 4,000 years. The original story wasn't written down. It was told from person to person for generations. And the story did not involve a spinning wheel, which wasn't invented until about 1000 BC. The little man was able to turn items to gold on his own.

105

The spinning wheel, which was used to spin flax into clothing, eventually became an important part of daily life for people all over the world. Spinning was a long, boring chore, and the people who had to do it told stories to pass the time.

The story of a helper with a secret name was told in many cultures, including cultures in Europe, Asia, the Middle East, and South America. Details of the story vary from place to place. But they always revolved around a magical little man who helps a girl and then demands her firstborn child. In the English version of the story, the little man is named Tom Tit Tot. He's called Titelli Ture in the Swedish version and Whupity Stoorie in the Scottish tale.

Brothers Wilhelm and Jacob Grimm first published *Rumpelstiltskin* in 1812. In this version the girl is told she must turn straw into gold. No spinning wheel is involved. She learns the little man's name from the king himself, who tells her a story about seeing the man singing in the woods.

At the end of this story, the queen says Rumpelstiltskin's name and the little man runs away. He is never seen again.

The brothers Grimm revised the story later. They added the spinning wheel. One version of this story ends with everyone in the court laughing at Rumpelstiltskin after he stamps his foot through the floor.

In 1857 the brothers published their final version. In this story the queen secretly sends out messengers to find the little man's name. The ending is more harsh than previous versions. When she says his name, Rumpelstiltskin stamps his foot through the floor, gets stuck, and tears himself in two.

Rumpelstiltskin has been retold countless times since the Grimm brothers' final version. It has been adapted into new stories as well, including in literature, TV, film, and even songs. Recent examples include the TV series *Once Upon a Time* and the *Shrek* movies.

OTHER PATHS TO EXPLORE

1. Rumpelstiltskin tries to take the queen's child, but he also saves her life three times. He even gives her a chance to get out of her agreement. Do you think Rumpelstiltskin is a good or evil character? Why?

2. How would this story be different if it were told from the miller's perspective? What does he have to gain by boasting about his daughter?

3. *Rumpelstiltskin* was originally told from person to person over several generations. This caused the story to change over time. To find out why, form a circle with your friends. Whisper a silly sentence into one friend's ear. Have that friend whisper the sentence to the next person and so on until the last person hears the sentence. How did the sentence change? Why do you think this happened?

READ MORE

Gunderson, Jessica. *Frankly, I'd Rather Spin Myself a New Name!: The Story of Rumpelstiltskin Told by Rumpelstiltskin.* The Other Side of the Story. North Mankato, Minn.: Picture Window Books, 2016.

Marsico, Katie. *Magic Monsters: From Witches to Goblins.* Monster Mania. Minneapolis: Lerner Publications, 2016.

Shurtliff, Liesl. *Rump: The True Story of Rumpelstiltskin.* New York: Alfred A. Knopf, 2013.

INTERNET SITES

Use FactHound to find Internet sites related to this book:

Visit *www.facthound.com*

Just type in 9781515787754 and go.

LOOK FOR ALL THE BOOKS IN THIS SERIES:

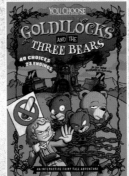